KBREAUN SHARPE

RELEASING GUILT
TO WALK IN PURPOSE

Pearland, TX 77584
www.kabeskorner.com

Printed in the United States of America

2025

To my husband,

Thank you for being my safe place and strength to do this work. I am forever grateful for you.

Contents

This Wasn't Part of the Plan

Moments in life compel us to pause, reflect, and question whether we are truly living in alignment with the life we are meant to lead. Most people feel this after a crisis or emotional breakdown. But for me, it's happening amid the build-up, during a time when I am juggling multiple roles and wearing countless hats. On the surface, everything looks like a success story—as I'm thriving, and inspiring others. Yet beneath the surface, there's a quiet whisper urging me to slow down. It's as if my soul knows that if I don't heed to this call. If I keep pushing beyond my limits. The weight of it all could come crashing down in ways I might not be able to control. On the surface, I marked the past few years with major milestones like the beauty and vulnerability of marriage. I started a private practice and left a business I founded with a dear friend. But beneath these outward changes was a deeper, more personal reckoning. A reckoning with my identity, my faith, and the patterns of responsibility and self-sacrifice that had shaped so much of my life.

This book is the story of that pruning process. It's about learning how to discern when a season has ended, even when it's painful to admit. It's about releasing guilt, which keeps us stuck in roles and relationships God has asked us to lay down. It's about trusting a loving God who doesn't waste our pain, but repurposes it to something far better than we imagined. Discerning when to walk away isn't easy, and letting go can feel like losing yourself. But I discovered that these steps, as hard as they seem, are the very ones that lead us to freedom.

I hope that through these pages, you'll see pieces of your own story.

Are you the eldest daughter? You work hard to balance your career, family, and personal life. Yet you wonder when you'll truly feel seen and cared for?

Are you a new mom? You hold it all together in silence, yet you feel guilty for needing rest, help, or just a moment to breathe.

Perhaps you're the one rewriting the rules. You're thinking twice about going home for the holidays.

You're tired of shrinking to keep the peace. But you still wonder if choosing distance makes you disloyal.

Maybe you find yourself wanting to leave a relationship or a job you've stayed in for years. Still, you hesitate, unsure if it's the right time or afraid that letting go won't lead to something better.

Not quite? Okay. You already hit your limit. You said what you swore you wouldn't. You cut them off or walked away, and now you're deep in the aftermath. You feel the ache of transition—but you're done settling for less than peace and respect.

Whatever your story, I want you to know this: You are not alone. God meets us in that tension, in the uncertainty, in the quiet undoing—and gently leads us to the other side.

This is the story of a hard but necessary surrender. It's about laying down what no longer aligns to make room for what does. Walking away may feel like an ending, but it's an act of faith that opens the door to God's divine purpose. I can't promise the steps will be easy, friend, but I can promise they'll be worth it. Welcome to this shared space.

"Sometimes the greatest growth begins in the disruption of everything we expected".

Before the Release

CHAPTER 1

The silent expectations I felt as the eldest daughter of seven took a toll on my well-being. Flashes of a major crisis would engulf my mind as I mentally prepared to take a call from a loved one. With a cut to the chase attitude, I asked, "What's wrong?". It's my mom. I already know it's not small talk. Maybe the car won't start. One of my younger siblings is acting up. Maybe she's overwhelmed with bills or just needs someone to vent to. I was used to putting out fires and anticipating needs. All while juggling texts and calls from three buzzing phones on my desk. *How am I even managing all this?* I muster up the energy to offer her encouragement. I don't get a chance to process before my sister texts, *"Ma was tripping—do you think we can come out there with you for the summer?"*. I'm trying to live up to being "the responsible one". I learned to serve others well. These expectations felt normal for so long. But I started to see how they were draining me. And though I love them deeply, there are days when I wonder—*who do I call when I'm the one unraveling? Because I am.*

I prep my work bag and head to the business I founded with my friend. I arrive and sit in the car. The engine still running, trying to stomach the guilt that's rising in my chest. Guilt for even considering walking away. I have a client session in thirty minutes. I haven't eaten today. My head aches, my heart's racing. Did I mention I have a full-time job I juggle during the day? I whisper to myself, *Deep breaths. You got this.* But the truth is—I don't want to go in. I don't want to keep pretending. Customers in the waiting room in awe of what we created. Phones ringing. Services are happening. Lives are being helped. But behind that front door, I'm not just the co-founder. I'm the biller, the admin, the support line for the team. The one catching every missed detail, refining our processes, to keep the whole thing afloat. All while quietly falling apart. I want to call my husband–for the fifth time today. But I can already hear the quiet disappointment when he finds out I haven't eaten yet. That was just enough to send me into an emotional spiral.

Getting married was a joyful sign of our togetherness. It began an exciting new chapter in our lives. *I found my person.* And yet, I'm navigating the unexpected grief of letting go of a version of myself that I had known deeply. There are very few married couples in my family. I learned a great deal of what not to do in relationships. From the importance of communication and respect. To the ways unresolved pain can ripple through a family. I longed for a sense of security and unity that my partnership would bring. At the same time, I felt unsure about how to build or sustain it. I prided myself on being self-reliant. I struggled with unrealistic fears about trusting my partner.

I didn't understand how much my last name defined me. It tied me to my family, my background, and the person I had fought so hard to become. A moment I remember vividly was rushing home to check the mail for my updated passport. To my surprise, they renewed it in my maiden name. As I sat in frustration, "Mad" by Solange came on my music shuffle.

You got the light; count it all joy.
You got the right to be mad.
But when you carry it alone, you find it only getting in, the way
They say you've gotta let it go.

Breathe, Kabe, I tell myself as I look over the name change form I messed up. My passport had always been my ticket to escape. From the weight of obligation and the constant demands of self-sacrifice. It represented freedom. A world where I could briefly put myself first. *No way I'm going to pull off a quick trip to Cancun now.*

I feel the pressure to be fruitful and multiply. And while I've watched friends' step into motherhood later in life– my body reminds me it's not that simple. The cysts. The irregular cycles. The discomfort I didn't have language for. I carry this tension of womanhood quietly. The nights curled up in pain. *Am I running out of time?* I try to quiet it, to bury it beneath my schedule. I'm too busy to slow down long enough to even try. It's just my husband and me here—no grandmas or "titi's" nearby to help. It's hard to name that grief when your life is full in other ways, but there's still a quiet ache for what hasn't come yet.

Love and loss, joy and sorrow—how could they coexist in such a moment of beauty? How was I going to surrender who I was, with so much uncertainty about who I needed to be to build a sustainable marriage? The pressure to be the perfect wife simmered quietly, while my husband only desired to give me a safe space to thrive. When I complained, he met me with open ears. When I cried at night, I awoke to handwritten cards. Flowers every Tuesday was the norm. When my food craving countered his Vegan diet, he sat with me at my favorite seafood restaurant. Even in his kindness, I felt shame. Trying to be everything for everyone else crowded him out of our sacred space. The space God graced us to hold for one another.

It all felt as if my heart was tending to a divided garden. On one side, fertile soil nurtures my cherry blossoms. They sprout vibrant and full of potential, urging me to grow stronger and more refined. To be balanced. To say "no". Eager for the soft girl life the girlies brag about. But on the other side, I'm tangled in an overgrown bed of thorny vines. The drain, fear, and obligation I feel are overwhelming. I'm pushing my limits. I'm maxing out credit cards to relieve the financial weight for others. I'm saying yes, even when it hurts my own well-being. If the vines of my old habits creep into my fertile soil, they threaten the space I need to thrive. For my flourishing garden to grow, I need the courage to clear away what no longer serves me. Then, I can nurture what brings life and renewal.

"Letting go doesn't start in our hands. It starts in our hearts".

Unpacking The Past

As I lay awake one night reflecting on the weight of it all, I remembered advice from one of my favorite podcasts, "The Basement with Tim Ross". He reassured listeners that "The kingdom of God is not a matter of talk but power" (1 Corinthians 4:20). When we feel lost, we should reflect on the last word we received from Him. I remembered a word I initially protested from my pastor a few months before. I stood at the altar full of anxiety and rage. Furious that I cared so much about everything and everyone. Pleading to God, I ask *why did you make me this way?* And hoped he was ready to tell me what to do now. My pastor laid his hand on my head with anointing oil. He expressed that God was doing a deep reworking in the seasons to come. Starting from the wounds of my childhood. *That doesn't make any sense,* I thought. Reflecting on my therapy journey, I felt confused that my work through past trauma wasn't good enough. I pride myself on being one of His strongest soldiers, but enough was enough. *But have you fully entrusted Him with your fears and the situations your troubled about?* I thought as I continued to lay in bed weary. I couldn't help but give a holy eye roll in joking protest. It was an uncomfortable truth from the Holy Spirit that I wasn't ready to hear.

Why did you make me this way? The question echoed louder again. It pulled me into reflection—into memories I hadn't touched in years. I pulled out my phone and scrolled through old Facebook photos to jog my memory. I found all the throwback gems my mom tagged me in. Images of my younger self began to resurface memories that shaped my beliefs about responsibility, loyalty, and self-sacrifice. I stared at an image of my family and me at my sister's Pre-K graduation. I was about 13 years old, standing with my sisters and twin siblings straddled on each hip, as I forced smile. I thought, *that was the day my mom wouldn't buy me that new backpack from the mall.*

As someone who prided myself on not asking for much, you tend to remember the few times you do. Especially when your needs go unmet. The picture took me back to 2008. I was at Fox Hills Mall with my mom. She is a resilient woman who had just finished her divorce from my stepdad. We were shopping for my sibling's clothes. I stopped to admire a window display at the Sanrio Surprise store. There it was—a pastel Hello Kitty backpack that stole my heart. I built the courage to ask her if I could have it. She promised to buy it for me if I continued to excel in school and help with the kids. That was enough for me. I worked hard, pushed through my responsibilities, and kept my end of the bargain.

A few weeks later, we walked past the same store, and the backpack was gone. Sadness bubbled up in my chest, and I couldn't hold in the tears. My mom noticed my mood almost immediately and asked what was wrong. I told her I was upset that, despite everything I had done, she never bought the backpack for me. Her response stopped me in my tracks. She leaned down, her tone both firm and weary, and said, "Girl. You don't get a reward for everything. Getting good grades is *what you're supposed to do*. Taking care of your brother and sisters is *what you're supposed to do*". She's an eldest daughter as well. I quickly dried my eyes. I thought, *Whatever. It's just a stupid backpack. My sister's shoes are more important*. I tucked the disappointment away, like I always did. Things that felt big to me, were small in the chaos of survival.

I swipe to another photo of me in colored skinny jeans and a lime green pearl necklace. New Boyz was playing everywhere back then. That morning, my mom woke us up early to go school shopping. But this time, I had a couple of hundred dollars saved from my summer job that took me three buses to get to. It's my freshman year, and I had to be fly. We go to Forever 21. I eagerly watched my clothes scan and drop into the bright yellow bag. I felt a sense of pride for my hard work. As I reached for my cash, I heard my sister yell my name as she bailed it to the counter with stuff in her hand. I glanced at my mom, hoping—just this once—she'd step in and spare me. She remained silent. So, I pulled out some clothes from my bag to trade them for hers. Giving up what I picked for myself just to cover the difference. "Fix your face! You're supposed to look out for your sister", my mom said. Her lips barely moved. But the wrong look from me cost even more. I tucked my chin as we headed to the parking lot. I'm old enough to catch one and be called "selfish like your daddy". A man whose struggle with substance abuse throughout his adult life, kept him from being in mine.

Why is it always me? It's never enough. All the babysitting, feeding, dressing, diaper changing, homework help, emotional caretaking, cleaning, and mediating were mine to bear. Somehow, I became the one who picked up the pieces day after day, as the weight of responsibility suffocated my adolescence.

As I continued sifting through photos, the memories sat with me. Not as a relic of guilt or regret, but as a point of curiosity. I'm sure my mother's goal was to instill responsibility. We had our share of difficult times. From moving a lot. The inconsistency of our father's presence. Relying on each other was our only strength. Passed down through generational survival. But what I internalized, was my value comes from how well I care for others. Doing for them is a duty, not a choice. I must be strong. My worth comes from hard work, success, or sacrifice — not simply being. This is just how life works.

These beliefs stuck with me as I grew. They became woven into my identity and shaped the way I approached everything—from school, relationships, work, and faith. It became a lens through which I saw the world. One that prioritized loyalty, responsibility, and self-sacrifice above all else—even when it came at a cost to me. I learned to work diligently and shoulder the weight with poise and grace. All while struggling with emotional loneliness.

We all carry our own version of the backpack story. We all have experiences, systems, and messages that shape the way we show up. We should explore how deep our beliefs are rooted. But we don't until we find ourselves in seasons of burnout. We wonder why rest feels like failure. In those quiet moments we linger in the car once we arrive home — trying to mentally prepare for what's ahead— we start to consider how heavy the expectations have become. But it's time to lean in a bit more.

After reading this chapter, I encourage you to pause, turn inward, and explore your core values and beliefs. You don't have to have all the answers, but curiosity is a powerful place to start.

What values and beliefs have shaped how you navigate life? *Ex. I have to be strong. People can't be trusted. Do something right or not at all.*

What sayings or mantras do you recall your parent(s) or caregivers referencing as a wisdom to life lessons?

What systems have you absorbed, often without even realizing it? Ex. *Don't let anyone see you sweat. You have to be twice as good to get half as much. If you want it done right, do it yourself.*

Do your values align with the person you want to be, or are they pulling you away from what matters most?

If you could rewrite one belief you hold about yourself or the world, what would it be, and why?

"You can't outrun
what you haven't
unpacked".

The Weight of Obligation

My disappointment about the backpack and looking out for my sister, was never about the money or object itself. It was about a desire to be seen. A desire for independence in managing my resources. For someone to say, "I notice your hard work and it matters". To have the choice in how I make decisions. These are normal conflicts within our development. The way our parents support and guide us through these conflicts play a crucial role in shaping our identity, building security, and what we learn about the world. If we're taught to show up from a place of fear and obligation, the desire becomes grounded in people-pleasing. The belief system I grew up with told me that love was earned through effort and sacrifice. The beliefs shaped my way of thinking and approached relationships, work, and faith as an adult.

Godly Stewardship and People-Pleasing

Godly stewardship and people-pleasing look the same on the surface but come from entirely different places. Godly stewardship is rooted in love and purpose. It involves a balance of the time, money, and talents God blesses us with. When we give through spirit led guidance, such as prayer. Our seed brings lasting good rather than reinforce unhealthy patterns in others. We don't feel resentful in this type of giving. We usually feel good as our seed or small sacrifice makes a meaningful difference in someone else's life. The Bible tells us God loves a cheerful giver (2 Corinthians 9:7).

People-pleasing is different. It prioritizes what others expect of us. It is a reactive response to helping others, born out of fear and the need for acceptance. We often show up to avoid conflict, rejection, or disappointing others. We say "yes" not because we have the capacity. But because we're afraid of what a "no" might cost us. People-pleasing tells us to keep sacrificing and keep giving. Over time, we start to measure our worth by how much we can do, fix, or sacrifice. The Bible reminds us that we can't fully serve God and live for the approval of people (Galatians 1:10). When fear drives our giving, it is no longer surrendered to God— but to survival. We are to serve Him with clarity, not codependence, which prioritizes our effort to stay connected to others instead of staying aligned with God.

- **Godly Stewardship** comes from love, seeking God's will, and trusting His plans. It values thoughtful actions led by wisdom and prayer.

- **People-pleasing** comes from fear. There is pressure to prove loyalty, striving for approval, and trying to control others' opinions. It leads to overextension, self-sacrifice, guilt, and burnout.

For a long time, I believed that Godly stewardship simply meant giving when there was a need. The more I give, the more like Him I must be. And when opportunities stirred something in me, I assumed that was confirmation to say yes. So, when a friend approached me to help start a business that felt meaningful, I didn't hesitate. At the time, I was deep in a waiting season for other promises that made me feel restless. I was eager to build and feel purpose again. The opportunity came felt like a door opening— to disrupt generational patterns and create the kind of stability I had only ever imagined. Like Martha, my commitment to service was deep. I was busy doing what looked like service and what felt like obedience (Luke 10:38–42). But underneath the hustle was a heart weighed down by worry, striving, and unspoken expectations.

In the early stages of business, the nudges from the Holy Spirit were apparent. I remember those property tours, feeling uneasy about going so big, so fast. I understood the kind of time, energy, and financial weight it would take to sustain it, and I suggested we consider smaller options. But my suggestions were seen as fear. Luke 8:15 reminds us that it's not just about hearing God's word. It's about receiving it fully, holding onto it, and being patient enough to let it bear fruit. But apparently I needed to have more faith. And though my spirit felt unsettled, I kept moving forward—out of duty than peace. After everything I had already invested. Backing out felt like failure, or a lack of faith. Even I struggled to trust the nudge fully.

You're probably asking yourself—If you felt all of that, why would you go forward anyway? Because this is the tension many women of faith quietly carry. When you've been taught that service is sacred, it's hard to tell the difference between surrender and self-sacrifice. Sometimes we say yes, not because we're at peace, but because we're afraid that saying no means we're not faithful enough. How many times have you called something faith when it's really you trying to make something happen on our own? We go into debt, stretch ourselves thin, and tell ourselves it's the cost of doing business. But deep down, I had to ask—if this was really from God, would it come with so much pressure and confusion? And just like Jesus gently reminded Martha, I had to learn that presence was greater than performance. That sometimes, sitting at His feet is the assignment. Everything else can wait.

In my striving to do more, I gave less to what mattered most. I prayed less and a wall slowly started to build in my marriage. Evenings felt rushed and our conversations were brief. The simplest request from my husband felt like one more thing I have to do. On a long list of other people's needs. I couldn't sit still long enough to let him finish a thought. The intimacy of our early days felt like it was slipping away. Couples counseling sessions became another box to check off. Rather than intentional work to build a strong foundation. The topic of priorities came up often. "I know you mean well" my husband told me. "But I want us to give the best of ourselves to one another. Not just what's left after you give to everyone else". His words stung. But he was right. Overextending myself was second nature to me. I never considered the toll it could take as we were trying to build. This was the generational pattern I needed to break.

Godly stewardship is understanding that everything we have—our time, energy, resources, even our relationships—belongs to God. This perspective calls us to seek His guidance before we commit, before we give our yes. I'm not talking about the "please God, let this work" prayer we whisper after we've already overextended ourselves. I'm talking about the quiet discipline of pausing first. Prayer and fasting. What's ordained by Him is worth the wait.

That kind of stewardship doesn't just shape what we give—it reshapes how we respond. Reflect on this practical boundary called "The 24-hour rule". Before giving your response. Taking this pause allows you to invite God into the decision. Reflect on whether the request is something you can take on, to refrain from reactive choices driven by obligation. This space doesn't just benefit you—it gives others time to explore alternatives as well.

Obligation says, "You owe them".

Obedience says, "You trust Him".

The Burdens We're Not Meant to Carry

Tying your self-worth to how much you can do for others sounds ridiculous to say out loud, right? But think about it. How many times have you taken on more at work? Felt afraid to call off when sick? Doing too much in dating relationships? Pressured yourself in the gym to look a certain way? Hoping that in doing so, you'll prove your value or feared not being chosen. It's not a conscious belief, but it's there—in the choices we make, the way we rank others over ourselves, and how we struggle to stop and rest.

Another hard truth is that most people won't stop you when we overextend ourselves. They may continue to let you pour, to give, and even overextend —because it may benefit them. They are used to seeing you carry it all. They may reinforce the idea that you should keep going, that it's your duty. This is why taking time to discern the weight you feel with God is crucial. God never intended for the burdens He places in our heart to destroy us. If they are, we must reflect on whether these challenges are truly refining us and strengthening our trust in Him.

I remember the summer I packed up my car and left everything familiar behind. I made the decision to move across the country for graduate school. The numbers didn't add up. I had barely enough in my checking account to cover the first month's rent, and there was no safety net waiting under me. When I considered staying for a local program half the cost and time, the discomfort of staying grew heavier.

My boyfriend at the time promised to drive with me to Texas. But he broke up with me days before the trip. It's my fault, I thought. I wouldn't nudge to the idea of staying. But the "on and off" again nature of our relationship wasn't going to cut it. With as much as a quick tune-up from my pops and a last-minute ask for my mom to join me, we set out that evening. Driving down the highway felt surreal. The sun hovered low on the horizon, painting the sky in strokes of orange and pink, its light bouncing playfully off the rearview mirror. My little car was notorious for running hot on long trips. But what were my options? Every creak of my car's suspension was a reminder of just how much I was carrying—not just in boxes but in responsibilities, hopes, and fears. I was eager for a fresh start, but it all felt miscalculated. With each mile, I had to remind myself to unclench my grip on the steering wheel and steady my breath. I prayed quietly as the road stretched endlessly before me, asking not just for provision but for peace in the uncertainty.

When I arrived in the peak of the Texas summer, 'better days' felt like slow passing hours. I found myself waiting for the coastal breeze that once came every evening like clockwork. But this transition was a bit different. There were months I didn't know how I'd pay the next bill, but manna seemed to fall just in time. Whether it came in the form of my unexpected academic scholarship, a kind word from a new friend, or a door opening at the right moment, those provisions renewed my strength. They reminded me that I was where I was supposed to be. But still, there was a lingering pressure in all my stretching.

I started a new chapter, but the same problems persisted. I never stopped fulfilling duties from home. From late-night FaceTime calls between time zones for homework help. To mediating conflicts about my four siblings sharing space in one bedroom. From making sure chores were done and the house was in order before my mom came home—just to keep the peace. I pitched in when I could, even if it meant stretching my own financial aid. I was the college advisor for my sister's school applications and FAFSA forms. When the new school year rolled around, I contributed what I had so they could get new clothes and supplies. It meant so much to me that my siblings felt confident, even when we couldn't afford it.

When one of them started having issues with school attendance or got into legal trouble, I carried the shame. My mom never said it outright, but the insinuation was there—maybe if you were home more, this wouldn't have happened. It was as if my distance made me responsible.

Behind all of that was the emotional weight of caring for my mom. The calls about having to move again with no plan in place, stirred something deep in me. Getting ready for school in hotel bathrooms are memories I tried hard to bury. Back when I opted to stay with my grandmother or close friends in hopes of the stability I craved. But my mom felt betrayed. Her resentment for my tantrums when I had to come back home showed up in subtle jabs and long silences. I wasn't just the daughter who left. I became the one who abandoned her in her eyes.

Somewhere along the way, I became her lil friend. The weight of helping her process emotional pain caused me to absorb it as my own. I believed I must protect her. You only get one mom. There's a strange shift that happens as daughters grow up. We start to see our mothers as full, complex women— flawed, human, and shaped by their own wounds. But closeness becomes tangled. What once felt like love and honor starts to feel like obligation, and emotional dependency gets mistaken for loyalty. So the more I tried to help, the more I carried. And the more I carried, the more invisible I became.

My understanding of obedience was distorted. I had confused it with endurance—believing that saying "yes" to God meant learning how to carry it all with grace, no matter how heavy it became. I was obedient to the call to relocate, but somehow the call disconnected on the part about laying things down.

The backpack I once wanted was now bursting at the seams. Straps digging into my shoulders. The load was overwhelming, but I saw it as a privilege. A sign that God trusted and blessed me because I could handle more. As He led me through this new chapter, I faced a hard truth about my obedience. I offered Him my "yes" with open lips, but my fists were still clenched—willing to follow, yet unwilling to release what was weighing me down. Obedience isn't just about saying "yes" to where God calls you. It's also saying "no" to what He didn't ask you to carry. In my spiritual immaturity, I had missed that. I feared that letting go of my roles meant failing or appearing weak. God's will must prevail—it's our refusal to lay things down that makes the journey harder than it has to be.

"Not everything
heavy is holy.
Some burdens
feel righteous
but are rooted
in guilt".

Loosening Your Grip

I still picture my first apartment in Texas sometimes, so bare and unfamiliar at first. It reminds me of how God doesn't call us to a place just to leave us there. He asks us to trust Him, even when our arms are empty, and we can't see how we're going to make it. Before He fills our hands, He calls us to lay something down—our comfort, the need to be seen, or the pressure to control outcomes we were never meant to carry.

So, friend, have you loosened your grip? Are you ready to release for what He plans to fill your hands with next? Obedience is less about what we carry and more about what we lay down. Yet, when we operate from a place of obligation, we can mistake them for acts of faithfulness. Could it be that all your striving is standing in the way of the surrender He's gently asking for?

Signs It's Time to Release and Trust

It's easy to blur the line between serving from a place of love or out of duty. Especially when you've been in that rhythm for a long time. Below are subtle but important signs that could mean you are operating from obligation rather than a heart rooted in His love and trust. What signs resonate with you the most?

- **You Feel Resentful** – the joy of giving fades, replaced by bitterness and exhaustion. God loves a cheerful giver (2 Corinthians 9:7), not one who gives from a place of guilt or fear.

- **You Prioritize Others' Needs Over Your Own Well-Being** – while selflessness can be honored, constantly neglecting yourself is not. Luke 5:16 reminds us even Jesus withdrew to rest and pray.

- **Fear of Disapproval Keeps You Stuck** – if your motivation is driven by the fear of what others will think rather than what God approves, you are trapped in people-pleasing rather than divine purpose (Galatians 1:10).

- **You Feel Drained, Not Strengthened** – serving in alignment with God's will brings renewal and strength (Isaiah 40:31). If you are constantly exhausted, it may be a sign that you are taking on more than you can carry.

- **You Struggle to Set Boundaries** – you feel guilty for saying no. But Jesus Himself set boundaries—He didn't heal everyone in every town or say yes to every demand. Learning to say no when needed is not rejection; it's wisdom (Matthew 5:37).

As you take stock of your heart and the reasons behind your actions, remember that surrender is not a sign of weakness but an act of trust in God's strength. Loosening your grip allows His purpose to take root, freeing you from the weight of unassigned obligations. When you lay down what no longer serves Him, your hands are open to receive the fullness of what He has in store. Trust that His plans are better than any outcome you could have controlled, and choose to walk in the freedom and grace He offers. His yoke is easy, and His burden is light (Matthew 11:30). Allow yourself to rest in that truth today.

"It's in the loosening of your grip, that you see what's been in your hand all along".

The Fear of Disappointing Others

Part of why we serve from a place of duty rather than love is the fear of letting people down. As a mental health professional and social worker, helping others has come with a unique blend of privilege and pressure. I am invited into the most vulnerable moments of someone's life, a sacred space where healing can begin. But along with that privilege comes an unspoken expectation—to have the answers, to ease their burdens, and to somehow make things right. While my work is meaningful, the fear of falling short was overwhelming in my first year of practice. What if a client doesn't see progress? This tension often pushed me into a cycle of striving, a need to prove my worth through results. But here's the truth I've learned, slowly and with much grace: I am *a vessel, not the source.*

The fear of disappointing others often feels most intense in our personal relationships. You might find yourself saying "yes" to plans or favors you don't have the energy for. You don't want to seem unreliable. You've taken on the burden of being the glue in your family. You feel responsible for teaching them better communication and how to handle challenges in hopes of ending toxic cycles. In your romantic relationships, you may be holding back your thoughts or needs to avoid upsetting your partner. These examples, though rooted in care for others, can lead to overextending yourself or burying your own needs. What if God is calling you to trust Him with these connections? Believing that honest, grace-filled relationships can grow stronger with healthy boundaries and vulnerability?

The Fear of Others Failing

Some fear of disappointing others comes from a strong belief that if we don't help, things will fall apart, or people will fail. If you're like me, it's almost unbearable to sit with the discomfort of seeing my younger siblings struggle to succeed. But if I'm not mindful, the discomfort leads to a compulsion to take control of situations. Have you ever gone in to support someone because you were afraid they might fail? One of my favorite metaphors to share with clients is, "A boat with a hole may still float". Even if someone seems flawed or lacks skills or knowledge, they can still function, survive, and move forward. Their methods don't have to look the same as ours to be successful. It's about balancing perseverance and allowing life's lessons to show us what to repair on our boat to grow and stay afloat. As we release the fear of disappointing others, we must also release the burden of outcomes we were never meant to control.

The Role of Grace

Shifting from the fear of letting people down to trusting in their strength doesn't happen all at once. It's an intentional choice made day by day, moment by moment. Grace is what helps us put the guilt we carry down—not in bitterness or frustration, but in the quiet assurance that God can redirect both you and those involved in the situation. Grace allows you to treat yourself with kindness and understanding. Even when you feel you've fallen short. It helps you release self-judgment and accept that imperfection is part of being human. In the words of my former professor, Brené Brown, "Authenticity is the daily practice of letting go of who we think we're supposed to be and embracing who we are."

What does Grace look like? In moments of doubt, I remind myself it's not my job to have all the answers. My role is to walk alongside my clients with compassion and do my best to guide them. The true work of healing belongs to God. I silence fear-based thoughts of, "What am I going to tell them?" to "God lead me to the words you need them to hear in this moment". This act of surrender has replaced my fear with peace. It's grown my comfort with stillness. Other strategies that may be helpful are:

- **Challenge self-criticism** and speak to yourself with kindness and compassion. As you would talk to a close friend.

- **Set realistic goals** for the time frame you are measuring to achieve them.

- Take time to **rest and recharge**, rather than push through and expect a quality outcome. You are tired! Self-care is essential, not selfish.

- **Forgive yourself** for past missteps and choosing to move forward instead of dwelling on regret.

- **Celebrate** small wins and acknowledge your efforts, even if the outcome isn't as expected.

Breaking Free

Letting go of fear doesn't mean turning away from the expectations placed on us. It's seeking guidance to discern which ones are truly ours to carry. And choosing to release the outcomes we were never meant to control.

At its heart, discernment is the practice of leaning into wisdom, not just knowledge. It is the practice of aligning our intuition, or Holy nudges we feel with God's truth. Wisdom grows when we approach life with a listening heart and stay teachable. It's in the slowing down where we can reflect on our experiences. It helps us see beyond charisma, charm, or pressure.

This type of wisdom comes from four main places—life experience from living. God's word where we find truth. The Holy Spirit who whispers that something feels off. From community and wise counsel whose insight helps us see what we have missed on our own. Here are practical ways to strengthen discernment and draw closer to God's wisdom.

- **Pray With Intention.** Make it a habit to bring your fears to God regularly. Honest prayers like, "God, I feel inadequate today. Please work through me and fill in my gaps with Your grace".

- **Ground Yourself in Scripture.** Martha's story (Luke 10:38-42) is one of my favorites from the Bible. A powerful reminder that being in "go mode" causes you to miss the work that pleases God.

- **Celebrate Progress.** Fear has a way of shrinking our focus to what's lacking. Take time to acknowledge your progress. Whether it's a small breakthrough or a single step of trust in God's process. These moments serve as reminders of His faithfulness.

- **Lean on Support.** Share openly with trusted people who will speak truth to your fears and remind you to return to God's guidance.

- **Set Boundaries**. You must set limits on what you can realistically take on. It might look like saying "no", even when you can show up but don't want to for rest and restoration.

Strengthening your discernment to manage the fear letting others down is a key first step. But what if you've set limits with others and it's just not working? You discussed your concerns with your loved ones or therapist, and they sense there is no more fruit from the relationship or opportunity. It's only leading to more chaos. Your requests are being ignored, and your boundaries aren't respected. Maybe you're like me. You started a business with a friend with clear goals. But over time, your efforts didn't match, and your visions changed. Your exhausted and your best efforts are met with resistance. You try to discuss it, but sense a lack of empathy or humility for your concerns. Friend, it may be time to rethink.

Grace allows us to recognize that walking away from an unhealthy situation isn't about giving up; it's about making space for what God has prepared for us. You have the right to change your mind or adjust the way you show up, if at all. But, how you do so matters. Grace acknowledges that we are human, with limited time and capacity, and that we cannot pour ourselves into every relationship, project, or opportunity without risking burnout or distraction from what God needs from you. Grace is on the other side of fear, where we meet the version of us that we desire to be.

"Sometimes it's not your failure you fear—it's theirs. But God never called you to carry what He alone can redeem".

When His Grace Lifts –
Knowing When to Walk Away

There's a weight that settles into your spirit when something no longer fits. It could be from a role you've outgrown, a relationship that feels strained, or a job that once brought joy but now leaves you drained. Walking away isn't easy, especially when you've invested so much into something. But knowing when to is a form of faith, and trust that His plans are better than anything you could plan to do alone.

For a season, the labor of my business was fruitful. But over time, things changed. The cracks in a foundation that was laid in haste started to creak. During meetings, I shared ideas to help us reach more people—things like offering new tools, training our team, streamlining processes to make services more accessible. But those suggestions were often met with rebuttal. Most of my ideas only moved forward if I took the lead on them. I started to notice a deeper issue—our commitment levels and values no longer felt aligned. The more I tried to build something meaningful, the more I felt isolated in the process. As I prayed through my decision, I examined the fruit of what we had built. In the couple years operating, customers showed up for the surface-level work, but none pursued the deeper work my team and I originally set out to offer. Despite my efforts to adjust our strategies and give grace, I did not see a pathway using the same tactics. "I thought putting the services together was enough. People just don't want it", my business partner would often assert. Slowly, my team began to leave. Bringing in new people that aligned with our mission became less of a focus. But even they drifted away just as quickly. Had our seeds fell among the thorns? Had the soil not been ready? (Luke 8:14). These were the questions I began to ask myself.

But at first, I ignored it. The uneasiness and constant fatigue. The quiet whisper in my spirit reminding me that submitting the business back to God started with surrender, not shame. I started to hold back on sharing my concerns. Not out of fear, but out of care. I didn't want to say anything that might cause them to feel ashamed or questioned.

The first few years of business are hard. You dive in headfirst, focused on keeping things moving. Before you know it, months have passed before you have a chance to come up for air and assess where you are. I convinced myself that tough seasons are normal and that pushing through was the price of success. I reminded myself that people were depending on me and that quitting wasn't an option.

But what happens when staying feels heavier than leaving? What do you do when God says to pause, but those around you want to make it happen on their own strength? I wrestled with guilt. The very thing that once felt like a divine opportunity, felt like a burden I was no longer graced to carry. I found myself back at His feet, asking, *"Lord, if this is Your will, breathe on it. If it's not, teach me to release it with open hands".* I had to face the truth. I was holding on out of obligation, not alignment. And something inside me began to shift.

I sat at the dining table. Shoulders tight and laptop open, staring at my wedding day screensaver. It had been just a few months after "the happiest day of my life". I thought, *why would I do this to myself?* I began drafting closure steps and transition plans like this was just business. But nothing about it felt simple. The words on the screen felt distant, like I was watching myself from the outside—exhausted and disappointed. A migraine pulsed behind my eyes, but I kept pushing— trying to make the exit feel smooth when everything inside me felt like chaos.

My phone lit up again. A missed call from my mom. Then a text from one of my siblings asking for help. I usually would've dropped everything to show up. But this time, I stared at the screen, frozen. *They know what's going on,* I thought. I was frustrated that my transition didn't seem to matter, as long as I was useful to everyone else. They knew I was stressed, but the gravity of what I was carrying didn't fully land.

I call a few loved ones and mentors my personal Board of Directors. Trust me—you *need* a handful of people you can bring certain things to. Trusted voices who remind you who you are and speak with the kind of wisdom that grounds you. Still, I wrestled with the fear of burdening them with my problems. Fasting and prayer tested my endurance. I questioned whether my efforts would make a difference. But it was my husband and Board who stood in the gap and lifted me up. That is the beauty of community. It's not about convenience. They didn't show up because it was easy. They showed up because they care. There's a balance. We give and take. Support and sacrifice go both ways.

Through prayerful discernment, counsel, and plenty nights sitting with my fears. I gained the courage and wisdom to do the hard thing. Stepping away from that business partnership became one of the most freeing decisions I had ever made. I realized that the work wasn't necessarily bad. Neither was my business partner. But God was calling me to something different. In trying to hold on, I was resisting His direction. I trusted that my obedience wasn't just about my release. But clearing way for what God wanted to do next with the business.

Signs God is Closing a Door

Recognizing that it may be time to walk away starts with subtle nudges. The signs aren't obvious at first. But as you lean into prayer, you'll begin to sense them more clearly. Here are a few other markers that could mean God is closing a door in your life:

- **His Grace Lifts.** Have you noticed that tasks that once felt effortless now require a lot of emotional or spiritual effort? Even small things can feel more difficult than they used to.

- **Closed Doors & Unusual Resistance.** Not every challenge is God closing a door. But if you keep hitting the same wall, no matter the different ways you try to move forward. Opportunities fade.

Relationships start to feel transactional. It might be time to seek God's direction (Revelation 3:7).

- **Lack of Peace and Internal Restlessness.** When God is trying to remove you from a situation, He will remove the sense of peace you once had about it. If you're feeling uneasy, drained, or disconnected, this could be a cue that God's grace has lifted (Philippians 4:7).

- **Conviction Through Prayer or Scripture.** We too often delay transitions waiting for a clear sign or prophecy. But God has already spoken through His Word. Passages you've read dozens of times might take on new meaning during seasons of transition. You may feel a conviction during prayer to release what you've been clinging to (Psalm 119:105).

- **Confirmation from Others.** God may use loved ones or spiritual leaders to affirm what He placed on your heart. Proverbs 11:14 reminds us, "Where there is no guidance, the people fall, but in an abundance of counselors there is victory".

Discerning what to do may not come right away when we reach the fork in the road. Walking away from the familiar— whether it's a business, a relationship, or a job. All boils down to having faith. If you're standing at the edge of a decision, remember that only God sees the full picture. He knows what's on the other side of every door, even when you can't see it. We must learn to sit with uncertainty. Trusting that clarity will come in God's timing. Isaiah 40:31 reminds us, "Those who wait for the Lord shall renew their strength".

"Grace covers us until it calls us forward. Staying too long can cost more than leaving".

Releasing Guilt and Trusting God's Plan

So, you've done the hard thing—you've ended the relationship, or resigned from your job. You've set boundaries with loved ones to restore trust and respect. But now the weight of guilt has crept in, making you question everything. Your heart may feel heavy with thoughts like, "Was I too quick to leave?" or "I feel so bad for hurting them". You may replay conversations in your mind. You wonder if you could've done something different to make it easier. That, my friend, is the exhausting voice of guilt whispering lies.

Many of us hold onto guilt not because of what we did—but because of what others *didn't do*. This kind of guilt is sneaky—it feels *righteous*. The anger you feel when someone hasn't taken accountability or owned their part. It seems like a simple, "I was wrong", could fix everything. The deep desire to hold others accountable actually prevents us from releasing guilt. Your thoughts during this time may sound like:

- *"If I walk away, it looks like I'm okay with what they did."*

- *"If I move on, I'm letting them off the hook."*
- *"If I let go, it means I'm the only one who ever cared or tried."*

Friend, you can't continue to over-carry what someone else was meant to hold. Healing begins when we stop waiting for someone to make it right and choose what makes us whole. If we don't, we stay in the cycle—carrying guilt, resentment, and a need for closure that never comes.

At first, I thought making the decision to leave the business would bring instant peace or relief. But instead, guilt showed up first—quiet but heavy. Then came the reactions from others. The kind of people whose opinions you don't even hold close. Yet somehow, their discomfort with my decision triggered mine. Before I knew it, I was over-explaining, trying to justify a decision that God had already affirmed.

My character and motives were twisted. My efforts over the years were dismissed, as though my decision was short-sighted. The shaming, guilt-tripping, and contempt burrowed deep into my heart. I felt quite worthless during this season. *If I let go now, I'm the only one who will ever carry the weight of what happened,* I thought. But that felt unfair.

I wish I could say I handled it all with perfect grace. But the truth is, there were moments my flesh took over. I said things I later had to pray about. I wanted to defend myself, to make sure they knew I wasn't the one to play with. And for a while, setting the record straight felt more satisfying than silence. But overtime, something shifted in my heart. Grace reminded me that while I felt hurt by the criticism. Others are also wrestling with their own pain, loss, and confusion that my departure symbolized. Eventually, I grew tired of letting the enemy bait me into cycles that left me feeling empty and ashamed.

One of the hardest parts of obedience is that others may not understand it. They might question your decision or imply that you've made a mistake. And when that happens, guilt tries to creep in, making you feel like you need to go back and "fix" things. But obedience isn't about pleasing others. It's about trusting God and walking in alignment with His will.

Jesus modeled obedience even when it was painful. When He prayed in the garden before His arrest, He honored that it was "Not my will, but Yours be done" (Luke 22:42). His obedience redeemed us, even though it cost Him everything. Reflecting on my struggles in relation to The Ultimate Sacrifice, helps me see them more clearly. You, too, have obeyed His call. You've chosen faith over fear, surrender over striving, alignment over obligation. Every step you've taken toward the freedom He's offering is a declaration of trust in His plan for your life.

Leaning into Grace

As you pull away from the guilt of leaving a situation, lean into the fact that God's love was never conditional upon you getting it right every time. It's easy to be hard on ourselves when we've stayed too long in a situation or don't recover as quickly as we think we should. But He loves you simply because you are His. Grace is God's love and forgiveness for us. Yet, we often forget to show that same kindness to ourselves. God's grace meets us in that messy, vulnerable space with unwavering kindness.

I think back to when I met my husband. It was during a time when I was battling uncertainty with my business, weighed down by debt, and struggling with poor eating habits that left me much heavier than I am now. And here's the kicker—he's a vegan! Doesn't God have a sense of humor? For some time, I struggled with my own worthiness for his kindness, because I didn't have it all figured out. Yet, even in the chaos and imperfection, His love and grace shone through. So, I want you to consider these reminders as you release the burden of guilt to lean into His grace.

- **Revisit God's Peace.** If doubt creeps in, remind yourself of the peace that came when you made your decision. Isaiah 26:3 tells us, "You keep him in perfect peace whose mind is stayed on You, because he trusts in You."

- **Release the Need to Justify.** If you share your experiences with others, remember you don't owe anyone an explanation for following God's call.

- **Surround Yourself with Encouragement.** Proverbs 11:14 reminds us of the strength in wise counsel. Surround yourself with friends, mentors, or a church community that encourages you in faith.

- **Pray for Continued Trust.** Tell God about your guilt and ask for help to release it. Psalm 55:22 reminds us to, "Cast your burden on the Lord, and He will sustain you; He will never permit the righteous to be moved."

"Guilt will keep you stuck in what was. Trust invites you into what could be".

Navigating Uncertainty

God's grace meets us in the mess and reassures us of His love. But trusting in that grace brings us to the hardest part of surrender—the in-between. Where you've released, yet wait in uncertainty for what God has prepared. You've jumped, but the safety net still hasn't appeared. Uncertainty triggers our core desire for security. We want to control things because it gives a sense of safety. When things are predictable, we can prepare. When they aren't, our limitations become clear.

I can hear the scoff you're going to make when I say– uncertainty is part of the healthy balance in our relationship with God. But it's true! It reveals how little control we actually have. It reminds us that we have limits. We can only map out so many details to guarantee an outcome. While it feels uncomfortable, it's an invitation to rely on the One who is in control.

When I made the decision to leave my business, I couldn't predict how everything would unfold. I knew I had to find a new office for my practice and worried the change might overwhelm my clients. I didn't know the first thing about what it took legally to leave a business. It was a season full of questions with very few answers. I am just a girl, okay! I hired an attorney to navigate the legal matters of the transition. I focused on handling unfinished business. Honoring contracts. Helping team members transition out with clarity and care. I found space to re-discover other parts of myself outside of work. I leaned into my hobbies and found that I really enjoyed creating things. I uncovered a passion for curating wellness events for women experiencing similar challenges. I DIY-ed all the backdrops and decor, which not only brought me joy but renewed my sense of purpose. I was also doing quiet work— untangling the weight of unspoken family expectations and learning how to say no without shame. In hindsight, I realize that even in uncertainty, God guided me. He used that time to shape me and reveal the next chapter of my life.

God never asks us to have it all figured out. He invites us to let go of trying to control what we can't. We should trust Him to guide us through uncertain times. So, let's explore the parts of your life where uncertainty feels difficult to navigate. Is it a career decision? A relationship? Your future as a whole?

Write them down. Next, I want you to take one step toward trusting Him with what you can't yet see, as we walk through real-life steps to move through uncertain seasons.

- **Bring Your Fears to God.** It's natural to feel anxious about the future. But instead of letting your fears run wild, bring it to God in prayer. Tell Him how you feel. Ask for His peace and guidance.

- **Close with Integrity.** Strive to leave things better than you found them. This includes completing work projects, handing off tasks, returning items, and having honest conversations before you depart.

- **Lean on Community.** You don't have to face uncertainty alone. Share your burdens with trusted friends or mentors who can pray with you and encourage you in your faith.

- **One Step at a Time.** Focus on what you can do, no matter how small. Your next step could be to update your resume, check your finances, dive back into a hobby, or reflect on the success of your previous endeavor.

- **Therapy.** Speaking with a professional may help you sort through difficult thoughts and emotions. It can help you identify next steps.

Not feeling certain about what is next is very uncomfortable. But growing your capacity for discomfort doesn't mean avoiding the hard thing or becoming numb to the tension we feel during this time. You must learn to stay present in it. One small shift that helped me grow my capacity for the discomfort of stillness was building in five-minute pauses between tasks. Not to scroll, not to plan the next thing—just to be still. To sit with my breath, check in with my body, or whisper a short prayer. Those quiet moments taught me that I didn't need a cleared schedule to find peace—just enough space to remember I am exactly where I needed to be within the reckoning. You don't need all the answers to keep walking.

"You don't need every answer to take the next step—just enough faith to move with God".

Becoming A Woman Who Walks in Purpose

There is something both exciting and terrifying about a new beginning or transition! Something shifts within us when we set boundaries, surrender what's beyond our control, and allow faith to lead the way. Taking up space for your needs may feel uncomfortable at first. But in time, you grow more comfortable. You become sensitize to old habits of putting everyone else first. So, when I felt ready to move again after leaving my business, I started showing up for myself in a new way.

My keys jingled in my hand as I unlocked the door to my new office. It was quiet— just me, God, and a room full of fresh possibility. I placed my bag down and whispered a prayer of thanks. This time, I wasn't dragging in what He told me to leave behind. This fond moment of pride slipped into grief as the day progressed. Crying one minute, zoning out the next. I stood on a step tool reaching down for the last bit of wallpaper with shaky hands. My friend could tell I was out of it. *I'm really doing this all over again.* I thought. From a 2,000-square foot business. To a

600-square-foot office. Thousands of dollars gone. I barely had the energy to explain what I wanted, but my girl understood. I stepped away for a quiet moment to reflect. *The steps back are part of the dance. To a rhythm of grace. Not defeat, I reminded myself.* As long as I'm where He needs me. I'll be alright.

My husband and I took a walk later that evening after hanging the last bit of artwork. The air was quiet, but my thoughts were loud. I finally said it out loud—I'd been blaming him. For the slowing down. For the stillness I didn't know how to sit with. I told him about the grief and guilt. How I'd let the weight of transition turn into frustration. How I made him the target when really, I was struggling to let go. He didn't interrupt. He didn't try to fix it. He just listened.

And in that quiet, I felt something shift. His steady presence through each aching day, reminded me of what I had forgotten. That I didn't have to earn love through exhaustion. That I was still worthy, even when I wasn't holding everything together. Even in rest. Even in grief. Even in the slow, uncomfortable work of becoming. What a Mighty God I serve. To redeem my trials and send me what I was unable to articulate as a need in its fullness. Our marriage began to grow in ways I only imagined.

With each client session, my guidance came from a different place. A place of tenderness. My trials had softened me, and were helping someone else find their way. I felt no need to hide my journey—I had lived through enough to speak with both compassion and clarity.

The ripple effect also showed outside the office. I stopped apologizing for my needs. Boundaries became more about choosing what's healthy than avoiding what's hard. As much as I've longed for more support from my mother, I've come to accept that she is doing the best she can with what she knows, and the cards that were dealt. Her love is never a question, even when it comes tangled in survival, silence, or fear. The tension in our relationship isn't just about what happened growing up—it's about what I hadn't yet allowed myself to feel. I buried those feelings to keep the peace, to stay strong, to protect everyone else. But holding space for her truth doesn't mean I have to silence my own. Healing required me to stop pushing those truths aside and start honoring them with compassion. There's room for both—gratitude and grief, empathy and boundaries.

God invites us to remain faithful in the tension, where obedience to Him may challenge the expectations of others. In a strange way, it felt easier saying yes to guilt than unraveling resentment for not choosing myself. I let people know how I wanted to be treated. For the first time in a long time, I believed I was worth honoring.

But the fear of uncertainty hasn't disappeared. It still knocks. But now, I do my best to pause—not panic. I look to God more often when I make plans. And when guilt starts whispering it's old lies. Telling me I've done too much, or not enough—I remind myself of the truth.

What does it look like for you to thrive from a place of clarity, conviction, and peace? To move or make decisions that align with God in purpose. Here are a few signs you're becoming that woman—not just surviving the shift, but walking in alignment with grace and grounded purpose.

- **She listens to conviction more than comfort.** You don't ignore the quiet nudges. You choose obedience over approval, even if it's inconvenient for others.

- **She makes peace with letting go.**
  You release what no longer serves you, because you trust God's timing more than your own plans.

- **She honors her values in real-time.**
  Your decisions reflect what you believe, not what you fear. You no longer feel pressure to explain your "no's". You trust it holds as much purpose as your "yes".

- **She invites God into her decisions.**
  You no longer make moves on logic or pressure. You create space to listen, to wait, to discern. Being in alignment is both strategy and spiritual sensitivity.

- **She embraces the becoming.**
  Walking in alignment isn't a one-time choice—it's a daily surrender. A daily return to the woman God is shaping in the stretch, and in the shift.

    As you prepare to move forward, I encourage you to take some time to reflect on your own story. Think about where your core values and beliefs originated. Be curious about the areas of your life where you are functioning outside of your bandwidth.

Where is God calling you to trust Him more deeply? What are you being asked to release? What is He inviting you to step into? What talents or interests have faded during tough seasons? Write these things down. Pray over them. Remember to focus on *just* the first step. Not the big picture.

For the woman thinking about leaving her job, it might be talking with a supervisor about your professional goals.

For the new mom, it might be reviewing daycare centers to imagine the help you need.

For the woman in an unfulfilled relationship, it might be journaling your desires for true companionship.

For the woman rewriting rules, it might be the phone call to tell them you won't be home for the holidays.

For the woman that already lashed out, it might be exploring, "What was I really trying to say beneath the anger?". Reach back out. Not with guilt, but honesty.

And for the eldest daughter, it might be the first no. *Even* if you can. Forgive yourself for being the one that made it out. You fought hard to be where you are.

And if you just *have to* let yourself worry. Do it when you have the feedback to make your next decision. In between time, focus on how you are one step closer to walking in alignment.

My hope is that you don't just see my story. We've walked through enough of my lessons to know I'm still figuring things out, just like you. But pull strength from it. Learn that it is okay not to have it all together. This is where the book ends, but it's where your next chapter begins. Go into it boldly. With a heart open to love, to creativity, to growth, and to purpose. Trust that God has been preparing you for this moment and that His plan is good. Submission looks like loosening our grip, repenting where necessary, and believing that He is faithful enough to redeem even the seeds we planted too soon.

If you do any looking back, think of how far you've come and the wisdom you have gained. From being tangled in guilt to walking in freedom. From clinging to the past to trusting in His perfect timing. Each lesson you've learned has prepared you for this moment. Each trial has refined you. Each step of faith has drawn you closer to trusting Him fully. Not only with the things we hold onto tightly, but with the future He calls us into. *Let it go.*

With every step
toward purpose,
she found herself
closer to the
heart of God—
less anxious,
more anchored.

About the Author

Raised in Los Angeles and now rooted in Texas, K'Breaun Sharpe is a licensed social worker, therapist, and writer whose journey has taken her across 13 countries. Her experiences across cultures have shaped her compassionate lens and deep commitment to healing. In 2022, she launched her private practice to help others thrive, blending her personal growth journey with her professional mission. Through her work and writing, K'Breaun empowers others to learn from the past, embrace new beginnings, and walk in clarity and purpose.

More Resources & Ways to Work with Me

This book is only the beginning. If Lessons from Letting Go resonated with you, there are more ways we can journey together:

Therapy & Emotional Wellness Support

As a licensed therapist, I support women navigating life transitions, emotional exhaustion, identity work, and faith-based healing. Explore additional resources designed to help you release guilt, set boundaries, and walk in purpose at **www.kabeskorner.com.**

Join My Community

Be the first to know about upcoming events, book signings, and women's wellness gatherings. Subscribe to my newsletter at **www.kabeskorner.com**

Invite Me to Speak

Interested in bringing this message to your church, podcast, or group? Let's create something meaningful together. Inquire at www.kabeskorner.com/contact.

Note from the Author

This book is a starting point, not a substitute for therapy. If something you read here feels especially heavy or familiar, I encourage you to seek support from a licensed professional.

Crisis Support (U.S.)

- **National Suicide & Crisis Lifeline**: Dial **988 -** 24/7 free and confidential support

- **Crisis Text Line**: Text **HOME** to **741741** Support via text message from trained crisis counselors

Find a Therapist

- **PsychologyToday.com** – Search for licensed therapists in your area

- **TherapyForBlackGirls.com** – Culturally competent care for Black women

- **The Loveland Foundation** – Free and discounted therapy support for Black women and girls through their Therapy Fund

No matter where you are in your journey, you don't have to navigate it alone. There is peace, purpose, and healing on the other side of letting go.